PRAISE FOR

THE STATE SHE'S IN

"Lesley Wheeler's poems call us to power and challenge us to own our dazzle even as they explore gradations of despair, as a woman navigates the Trump years, marching in a cold city 'pinked/by hats with pointy ears,' ever alert to her 'inhospitable secret vagina' and whether it will 'be grabbed or/ judged not fit for grabbing.' Wheeler's formal virtuosity wheels and sparks as she explores the impact of whiteness and sexism on the literal state—its history, its land, its educational institutions—she occupies. 'I need to learn/ how to endure my own bitterness,' she writes, as the contaminated water sings.' In a wallop of a poem, 'New Year's Colonoscopy,' she conjures: 'for I/boiled the bones and drank the steam,/sipped pink potions hours on end, emptied/myself of last year's toxic shit, and am clean.' Wheeler's research, her feral witchery, her poems themselves, are an answer, if not the antidote, to the state we're in."

—Diane Seuss, author of *Four-Legged Girl and Still Life with Two Dead Peacocks and a Girl*

"These poems showcase Lesley Wheeler's acerbic wit and vast intelligence– all laced over with a compassionate spirit for what divides us and what makes us whole. This gorgeous collection interrogates a landscape where a singular fruit makes 'seeds jingle. Custard's plush in the mouth,' while still hoping to arrive at a place where we'd prefer, '…the sparrow be true than cells struggling to contain unlikely radiance, and failing.' This is a collection of uncommon frankness, a poet of uncommon grace.

—Aimee Nezhukumatathil, author of *Oceanic* and *World of Wonders*

"What is the state of Lesley Wheeler's *The State She's In*? Accompany her there on her travels through history and culture, past and present, and you will discover more than you knew existed, including a spell for ridding oneself of certain politicians and a feminist bingo card. There's exuberance in these forms, humor in this self-awareness, and best of all, fierce compassion for the lost and downtrodden throughout this powerful, intriguing collection."

—Lisa Lewis, author of *Taxonomy of the Missing*

"The tinder of Lesley Wheeler's latest collection of poems ignites a tremendous bonfire with the glow of both history and the future illuminated in the present dark. In poem after exquisite poem she writes of both the spark and the ember, where 'Scent resonates/ even though the blooms are closed.' Here in her breathtaking work the landscapes of the past are indelibly linked with our hardwired present. And through it all, the defiance of the speaker evokes Lowell's stubborn skunks who turn their tails (and tales) against narratives that neglect to tell all but the most evident truths.

—Oliver de la Paz, author of *The Boy in the Labyrinth*

THE STATE SHE'S IN

The State She's In

Lesley Wheeler

Lesley Wheeler

© 2020 by Lesley Wheeler
ISBN: 978-1-943981-17-5

All rights reserved. Except for brief quotations in critical articles or reviews, no part of this book may be reproduced in any manner without prior written permission from the publisher:

Tinderbox Editions
Molly Sutton Kiefer, Publisher and Editor
Red Wing, Minnesota
tinderboxeditions@gmail.com
www.tinderboxeditions.org

Cover design by Nikkita Cohoon
Cover art "Censer" by Ida Floreak
Interior design by Nikkita Cohoon
Author photo by Kevin Remington

for the Nasties

CONTENTS

State Song	3
In the Pink	4
The South	6
Ambitions	7
Fifty-Fifty	8
Spring Rage	9
Occulted Sonnet	10
Traces	11
Uncivil	13
Journey	14
En Dehors Garde Bingo	15
Black Walnut Tree	16
Selfish	17
Fire Ecology	18
Dear Anne Spencer	20
Ambitions	21
Visibility Poor	22
American Incognitum	23
Before Lexington	25
Racketing Spirits	30
John Robinson's List, 1826	32
Bells for Henry Allen	34
"Recumbent Lee" by Edward Valentine	37
Five-Star Reviews of Lee Chapel	38
Boil-in-Bag	40
Paid Advertisement	41
State Roads	42
First Baptist, Lexington	43
Ambitions	44
This Has Gone On Long Enough	45
Postlapsarian Salsa Verde	46

Listen to the Mockingbird	47
Inappropriate	48
Rescue Ballad	49
Situation Room	50
Inside Out	51
Credit	52
Imperfect Ten	54
World Order	55
Hibernaculum	56
All-Purpose Spell for Banishment	57
It's Striking How Many People Lobby the Code	59
Invocation	60
Perimenopause	61
Song of the Emmenagogues	62
Millay at Forty-Nine	64
Turning Fifty in the Confederacy	65
She Will Not Scare	67
The Ferry	68
Says the Cab Driver of the Apocalypse	69
Energize	70
Old Bag	72
State Fruit	74

Ambitions 75

Evaporative Haibun	76
No Here Here	77
Insatiable	79
Meditation	80
Cave Painter, Dordogne	81
House Call	83
Pushing toward the Canopy	84
Spirals	85
Feeling Good	86
Border Song	87

We Could Be Cyborgs	88
Native Temper	89
Live from the Surface of the Moon	90
Illuminated	93
New Year Colonoscopy	94
L	95

THE STATE SHE'S IN

STATE SONG

Because I call you, wind strips trees
of brittle limbs they did not need.
The streambed tilts a muddy ear

and I pour words into its drain, the cup-
shape someone's heel dug filling up
as if with rain. Because I call us

together, the mountain blushes. A curtain
parts, loosens into rags of steam. Sun
and clouds pattern fields with roving

spotlights. Because I call you, power
thrums the ground. Now is the hour,
gilded, grand. I call this dazzle ours.

IN THE PINK

January, 2017

Independence Avenue is veiled
by TV screens. The platform is so
far away, it becomes fiction.
Mist never lifts from the tip
of the obelisk. Who could say

why I march, shivering,
through a city pinked
by hats with pointy ears?
My right hip throbs. Cold-
nosed women throng the streets.

One pushes me and I push back,
bracing around my panicked
child, grasping her hood
as the crowd surges against
barricades, unable to pour

itself down Constitution,
because that vessel brims
with more pinkness, milling,
unstill, right up to the Ellipse.
Cell service blocked, although

my phone offers to text pictures
to the Secret Service. No toilets.
No water unless wrung
from the air. Nor is any stalled
block indivisible: activists eye

each other's signs, veer away.
A penis with a comb-over.
A Woman's Place is in the Resistance
and Carrie Fisher's serious face
hoisted by girls in space-buns.

Trump and Putin making sweet
unlove. Countless cartoon uteri
lofted into polity: she, she, she.
Meanwhile, men orate.
This continues to be America.

Sometimes I join the chants,
disbelieving them. We
are not the same. A uterus
does not a woman make. Yet
my hand knots with my daughter's

on the way back to the bus
until we stop in a sandwich shop.
Gender isn't real! my rebel yells
as she reclaims the men's room,
emptying out her fear,

making space for reverie—flamingo
as a sunset, cherry as a blossom.
Knitting it would be beyond
me, but *you can write the poem,*
she says, *for my swearing-in.*

THE SOUTH

Once, you knew where you were going:
from winter's unambiguous branches
through flushing eastern redbud
toward the shabby linens of the South
bleaching on dogwood racks. Toward
manly honor and chaste womanhood,
dusted with gunpowder, shaded from heat
by genocidal legacies. Not so fast,
youth I was. Not so neat. Sure, the glass
of tea will sweat where tongues grow cool
and slow as minted bourbon. Sure, some
white shoppers won't stand in the black
cashier's line, allow his wrist's revolution
to float their collards or mayonnaise jars
over a scanner's bloodshot eye. The hate
you'll recognize, thinking you can stand
to one side. An innocent cartographer.

But malice won't sit where you mapped it,
emitting a predictable growl. Stop knowing
everything and look around. Hear,
above your banging pulse, an implicated
tune, weathered and blue, voice of land
pushed up sore, its grudges cold. Those notes
twist down piney slopes, fume into creeks
by whose banks the copperheads sun
like slippery hieroglyphs. They scrawl a tale
that had been camouflaged from you even
as you sang your lines. Now the story holds
you in its lap. Now it's poised to strike.

AMBITIONS

Liverpool

I. In '62, my young mother flew from known melodies, from clouds rolling up and down the Mersey with the tides.
II. Where would I be otherwise? Each curved person a lattice of contingency. Weak sunlight filters through.
III. She was born in a curved iron and glass shed, Lime Street Station platform eight for London Midlands, with a hissing exhale and a rocking momentum.
IV. Corridors of red sandstone, arched brick, concrete bearded with soot and moss. Four pairs of rails rusted pink. The city's muscles contract.
V. Towers topped with empty nests. Where are the birds?
VI. My return ticket bought by her departure. My diplomas. My pay stub. My upwardly-mobile American refusal to pick up after men.
VII. Brakes whine softly until the country opens and I pick up speed.
VIII. Far away, joint-sore, she is throwing off a duvet, opening blinds, creaking downstairs to her son's kitchen, listening to news of brutal collusions.
IX. Daisies, buttercups, yarrow—flowers that cannot be suppressed—and sheep-cropped hills beyond.
X. Clouds are heavy, sorrowful. They resist breakage but wind has its own ideas. Look at the azure vents it opens, with a tearing cry.

FIFTY-FIFTY

Odds are the ending's beginning
now. Your cheating father stumbles
into rising seas. History burns
and in the exhalations, ivy
ratchets up its poison. A beloved
child speeds off on a train and men
mishear your Title IX complaint.
Your third cat slinks away like smoke
while chemo ticks into your mother's
shrinking veins. Time to divest
yourself of puberty's gifts without
a thank-you card. Checks flutter off,
and samples in vials. Higher risk
of cancer, lower of ever forgetting.
Turns out your heirloom is worry
plus a taste for bitterness. So chance
a walk downhill through scattered trees
and consider what to give away
before you lose it. You're a specialist
in suspense, prone to read ahead,
yet the plot is running fast. A swarm
of futures mate at dusk by the river,
and all of them are betting on blood.

SPRING RAGE

All afternoon and evening, wrath boils
down the gutter pipe. In a sewerless
town, it foams across yards trashed
by dandelions and tiny violets,
crashes past curbs, and maps a sloping
path to creeks, polluted en route
by exhaust, soap, the ash of striving.
I am tin. I am flimsy and replaceable.
But by the coursing of anger I know
I am not clogged with leaf duff or dead
birds, I can carry a flow, I can talk
about its cool extraordinary passage.
Hollow but not nothing. A shape
that directs torrents down and down.
I want to say to the men who wrecked
my life, fixed my life, and are now
expecting gratitude: you cannot
break or repair me. But they are busy
in the clouds banging thunderheads,
directing water to fall, not understanding
how it will scorn their plans and their power,
displace who it wants, when it wants,
numerously, even if today it seems
invisibly biddable, whispering past us all.

OCCULTED SONNET

You
look,
crook
head
awry
to
elude
my

gaze.
Nobody
sees
me,
these
days.

TRACES

Some nights a train rattles past,
moaning, ghostly, although
the segregated station closed
seventy years ago. Relocated
brick by truck. Rails pulled up.
Ground misted with broken glass.

Our road used to lead to the depot.
A neighbor used to shiver
at her toddler's words: *This isn't our
house, the ladies in white dresses
told me so.* Unwilling to accept it,
photos slammed their faces down.

Once a stranger shaped initials
on our foundation. Now ligatures
crumble. Once a lilac was planted
to ward off spite. Scent resonates

even though the blooms are closed.
The sweetness says: no house is yours
or mine. Despite everyone's claims,
the lingering spectral whiteness,
nobody owns this beaded grass,
that vanished tree, tulips brooding
on sunny days past. The message aches

like the whistle of a phantom locomotive
or heart-of-pine floor crying out.
On some fraction of an acre, in the half-
familiar April rain, protest sounds.

This isn't your spring, the nesting
mockingbird sings. Just a spur
you can ride to the real connection.

UNCIVIL

The magnolia drops its anger pink by pink.
Eighteen-wheelers loaded with it rumble down interstates
aroused by their own dark momentum.
Cats rake claws through anger then nap on shredded upholstery.
Cables fizz high above gutters, looped and twisted, twanged
    by doves.
Flags snap in it. It propels the old woman and her encumbered cart.
A suburban circular. A city racket. A maritime breeze.
Some people give it away, but when they drive off
the cur follows, homing unerringly.
You don't love me, it snarls, but I will always want you.
Each cloud an anger of its own, dimming the alfalfa fields.
Some people exorcise it, smudging sage through anger's rooms,
rinsing walls with vinegar and bleach. They claim
to have forgiven anger. Burned it off. God or Clorox granted peace.
Look, no anger here, I'm not angry, that's not how I feel.
But you can detect the scent even on the street,
rising from his wool suit's weave, caught in her hair, samara's wing,
even in sighs, sick and sweet, since anger's born in the gut, feeds
on your nourishment, and you'll never in life starve yourself clean.

JOURNEY

Not the man who said, *Whoa, did I have a dream about you.* Nor the other who said, *We were so right to hire you, you get lovelier every year.* They just liked me stupidly. What altered my endurance, what crawled into cells and rewrote code, was slow dosing. The new dean changing clothes in the front office, blaming women in meetings, draped across their chairs. *Your colleagues seem to want you as head,* angling his height away. *Your report is late. Your new hire's a problem, how is she failing now? About that drunken abusive professor—your student lied.* None of it sounds like a regulated toxin. Then, in reply to contradiction, he began prodding my arm with a hypodermic finger under the table. I was paralyzed. Called for help and found previous complaints decomposed. Began then and there to metamorphose. Gave up my promotion. He chased me back to the tainted wood, made companions of those who liked me stupidly. Ailed in my burrow for years until one day I snarled and they were all surprised. I had become a wild animal.

>through late snow, wet boles,
>a red brush flames—she who
>disbelieves in spring

EN DEHORS GARDE BINGO

after Fatimah Asghar and Mina Loy

HITCH A RIDE HOME FROM THE FEMINIST BOOKSTORE WITH WOMAN IN RED PICKUP TRUCK	WRITE POEMS ABOUT YOUR RESEARCH INSTEAD OF ARTICLES	KEEP A STASH OF TAMPONS PAST MENOPAUSE BECAUSE A SISTER MIGHT NEED HELP	SUFFER NEURASTHENIA	RISES FROM THE SUBCONSCIOUS… CARCASS COVERED WITH BLUEBOTTLES (YOUR COUNTRY)
FALL SILENT BECAUSE YOU CAN'T SPEAK ABOUT THEORY UNLESS YOU 100% UNDERSTAND IT	MESSAGE ALLIES ON FB BECAUSE YOU'D RATHER BE SPIED ON BY RUSSIANS THAN YOUR BOSSES	COUNT CITATIONS & MAKE SURE 51% COME FROM WOMEN	ASK SOMEONE WHO PROMOTES HUMAN RIGHTS ABUSE TO LEAVE YOUR RESTAURANT	HIDE BECAUSE EVERYONE HATES AMBITION IN WOMEN, PLUS YOU NEED THIS JOB
INSIST GRIDS PERPETUATE THE PATRIARCHY & REDESIGN THIS BOARD AS A SPIRAL	SKIP MEETING BUT STEAL BOXED LUNCHES WITH A FRIEND & DISCUSS BODY DYSMORPHIA	**EPIPHANY: THERE IS NO FREE SPACE**	CREATE A TRAVEL GUIDE TO A PLANET YOU'VE NEVER VISITED	CALL OUT PANELS/ PUBLISHING VENUES POPULATED ONLY BY WHITE MEN
VOLUNTEER TO THROW WORK PARTY/ BRING BAKED GOODS THEN ASCEND INTO RAGE	RESERVE THE WORD "GENIUS" FOR PoC & WHITE PEOPLE WHO IDENTIFY AS WOMEN	TEACH BOOKS THAT SCARE YOU IN A GOOD WAY	BLIZZARD THE ATTORNEY GENERAL WITH SANCTIMONIOUS SNOWFLAKES	YOU'VE GESTATED FOR SO LONG— GIVE BIRTH TO YOURSELF
DISCUSS SEXUAL HARASSMENT IN A GENDER-BINARIZED RESTROOM	VOTE FOR CANDIDATES WHO DEFEND SOCIAL JUSTICE ENERGETICALLY	TELL THE LEAST SELF-CONFIDENT BRILLIANT STUDENTS THEY'RE BRILLIANT, CONVINCINGLY	LISTEN TO EVERYONE EXCEPT PEOPLE WHO DON'T THINK YOU HAVE A RIGHT TO SPEAK	REFUSE TO PLAY BINGO UNLESS EVERYONE WINS

BLACK WALNUT TREE

How do you persist, knowing
your shadow is poisonous?
How do you bear the thirst
driving your taproot through
silty clay, toward creek or sewer,
seeking more and more water?
The same power helping you
grow strong and straight,
heartwood densely grained,
leaflets velvet, serrate—
it pushes others away.
You deep-grooved volunteer,
magnificent citizen sickening
my yard: I need to learn
how to endure my own
bitterness. Tell me your tough-
shelled fruit and I will tell you
mine, as I render the earth
unkind. Chemistry of hunger,
ambition. Bound to harm,
whether or not we rue it.

SELFISH

The sun sinks down
or earth turns away.
These are words we've found:
a verb burns down
behind the mountain's noun.
But it's only what we say,
that the sun crashes down,
when really we turn away.

FIRE ECOLOGY

Before chemicals burn her scalp bald
as a cindery match head, she rattles
with fever. Gray-blond tree

clinging to rock, she'd weathered
extinction events. Eruption and
glacier. Scorched and quenched

as if by centuries. Thought herself past
cataclysm but there's always
another storm cloud hunching in.

Cancer jams her. Grips kidneys
and wraps hard around womb's gap.
What was freedom became kindling

for chemo's controlled burn.
She blazes in the hospital bed,
in my useless arms, naked shaking

scrap of flame wanting conflagration.
Here comes flicker and fall.
Pine smashing down mountainside

to oxidize on a valley floor where
leaf litter sips ice slow. The paradox
of life-out-of-death feeds bloodroot

striving through snowmelt. *Well,
I always wanted children*, she whispers
to the smoldering vista.

Antibiotics drip into a bruised arm.
The poisoned world all understory.
To need, the smoke resembles hope.

Love. *And look*, she says, *look at you.*

DEAR ANNE SPENCER

From cherry blossom season, I write
to inform you the parties are still
stupid here. Last night I succumbed
to cocktails at the book-strewn home
of a fund-raising politician, trim as a
tulip, who set out platters of shrimp:
pink fingers, crooked. High-ceilinged rooms
stuffed with old men gone septic
under buttons, under powdery cheeks.
Over tea in your garden, I'd say more,
but for now let's admit I was rude,
escaping through a racket of
invisible birds, finding a friendlier
table, nibbling syllables of cheese
with women in mourning, whose
joints are painfully inflamed.
I'm tired, Mrs. Spencer, of meanness
and NDAs. I wish I could bring by
some birdsong, or the rose-scented
quarrels of what I've been reading,
this rainy heap of magazines.
One hopes for a breeze, impolite,
rowdy, to rip the gorgeous petals
down. One hopes to be it. I'd pen
you a note from that town in pretty tatters.
Until then I am admiringly
yours, a flock of cedar waxwings,
a bristle of spears that would rather,
some unsecretive day, be lush
and ant-starred peonies. Sincerely.

AMBITIONS

Blue Ridge

I. Drift as Virginia once drifted from old certainties, cracking and packing up north.
II. When Africa skids in, accede to the crunch despite how it hurts. Lift up hands of basement bedrock in praise.
III. Erode. Let wind and water pour and rub, for they will wear you down with or without leave.
IV. Oak and hickory set up industry, blueberry and huckleberry ripening in the understory. Birds, bears, people.
V. Forget how the river was named. Forget what the namers called themselves. Daughter of the Stars is nostalgia's dream.
VI. Recall the Treaty of Lancaster, between the Haudenosaunee Confederacy and the colonial governments of Virginia and Maryland. In 1743, Governor Gooch gave one hundred pounds sterling, followed next summer by two hundred gold. The Scots-Irish thought that settled it.
VII. Great Path becomes Valley Pike becomes, in Lexington, Main Street. Hotels take root, branded for generals in a different confederacy. The Civil War, a marketing scheme. Reenact a microbrew in my piano bar.
VIII. Is this really where I live? Along Woods Creek, I listen to contaminated water sing.
IX. Aim low, sweet mountains, blue with arboreal hydrocarbons.
X. With notions my canoe is laden. I will not deceive you, I'm bound to leave you, but till then, don't look away.

VISIBILITY POOR

The first year was smoky. Milk, ache,
and a vague burnt tang, a granular
darkness somehow hanging in bright
air, cooling the underside of clover.

Could not think, straight or crooked.
Had to sleep for an age. Invisible
tail, broken by a babe's rough passage,
still throbs, still rues church pews.

And now as if some spark of grief
had smoldered in a cupped rock,
in a plush of ash, and woken again—
can you scent it? Animal self,

breasts hot, paces the edge of shade.
One child grew and left but may be
crying faintly, three hills away. Another
running hard out and back, training

for distance. The trees undress,
casting off scorched burdens, while I
become more vigilant, more choked,
each year, by a stinging haze of snow.

AMERICAN INCOGNITUM

Tusk, thigh bone, molars plucked from a sulfurous
marsh by troops en route from one fight to
another in 1739. Back then,
maps of the Ohio gleamed as blankly

as brains of trudging hungry men, meaning
not pure, not quite. Their pockets stuffed with acorns
and desire. Now local streets are blank, too,
a nearly naked parchment. Snow wants you

to forget the car, your feet. Opacity masses,
conspiring to white-out.
                        Those molars landed
in Cuvier's hands around the French Revolution.
Considering them, he invented an idea:

extinction. Acorn-brown, passed impossibly
down. Proof *of a world previous to ours.*
But he'd reject Darwin's *transformisme.*
Animals don't evolve, he thought. They just

disappear, lumbering free of history…
Giants, mammoths—you reconstruct the past
you need. For Cuvier, bloody overthrow.
For others, fantasies of continuity.

Or coexistence. Imagine mastodons
still shake the valley floor, ahead of hunters,
ice. Calves and mothers browse conifers,
exhale resin. It's confabulation.

Also, fragrant. Try to recall, while you crouch
in a renovated house, how they crash
along the road, stripping oaks. Listen
through your own bones: subsonic parley.

BEFORE LEXINGTON

Unremembered settlements

Vapor stole from the Maury River—
droplets deflecting light—
before this town was hammered out.
Algonquians and Iroquois

hunted in it, voices muffled
by clouds, words dissolved
among other, older words.
Until they sold the right, or

that's how governors told it.
Fog softened the land,
made it seem kind. Maroons
stealing themselves and their kin

fled to it, from eastern plantations.
Built tree-bough dwellings here
with liberated tools, sowed
salvaged corn, sang in languages

forgotten since by heron and crow.
The river a mercy. The mountains
a shield. Not a pottery shard
remains of them. Not a nail.

Mist assisted when militia came to kill
their leader, forced the others back

through passes in the Blue Ridge.
Then lifted its innocent hands.

Whiteness will not save you.
Warm water lifting into cold air
erases, always. This place,
this shine, wants you to forget.

Unremembered settlements

~~Vapor~~ stole ~~from the Maury River—~~
~~droplets~~ deflecting ~~light—~~
~~before this town was hammered out.~~
~~Algonquians and Iroquois~~

~~hunted in it, voices~~ muffled
~~by clouds, words~~ dissolved
~~among other, older words.~~
~~Until they sold the right, or~~

~~that's how the governors~~ told ~~it.~~
~~Fog softened the land,~~
~~made it~~ seem ~~kind. Maroons~~
~~stealing themselves and their kin~~

~~fled to it, from eastern plantations.~~
~~Built tree-bough dwellings here~~
~~with liberated tools, sowed~~
~~salvaged corn, sang in languages~~

forgotten ~~since by heron~~ and ~~crow.~~
~~The river~~ a mercy. ~~The mountains~~
~~a shield. Not a pottery shard~~
remains ~~of them. Not a nail.~~

~~Mist assisted when militia came to kill~~
~~their leader,~~ forced ~~the others back~~
~~through passes in the Blue Ridge.~~
~~Then lifted its innocent hands.~~

~~Whiteness will not save~~ you.
~~Warm water drifting into cold air~~
erases, ~~always.~~ ~~This place,~~
this shine, ~~wants you to forget~~.

Unsettled

stolen
    deflected
muffled
    dissolved

tell
    [what] seemed
mercifully
    forgotten:

this shine
    remains yours
and [mine]

    by force
erasure
    [theft]

RACKETING SPIRITS

Brownsburg, Virginia, 1825

She careened from kitchen house to dining room,
bare brown feet quick in the frosted yard, crying
of *the old woman with her head tied up*. Nobody's
chasing you, Maria, Dr. McChesney chided, helping
himself to a glistening slash of ham. His daughter
Ellen giggled and pinched Maria under the table.
Mean. Also eight years old but freckled as a biscuit.
Free. Maria cast a chilly eye on her, stepped away
from the fragrance bread makes when you break it.
Nobody's here, she thought, and soon you'll know it.

A few weeks later, charred rocks began to fall, deliberate
as fists, scorching hot. They volleyed against the roof,
blackened grass, cowed the family. Bewildered,
the McChesneys sent Maria to nearby cousins.
She strolled the miles so slow she could almost see bloom
come to the Judas trees, till the final rise. Then twitched
and charged, wailing of witchery. She found the Steeles
already stirred, starring the lawn, their backs to her,
as they stared toward a clatter in their house. A peek
showed furnishings piled up like sticks, of a sudden,
in the parlor, cupboard glass smashed by stones
from nowhere. Mr. Steele commanded her back home.

Now the whole county gossiped. Mischief likes
ventriloquy. If Dr. McChesney peered out the door,
earth-clods pummeled him. His sister, Miz Steele,
kept visiting even when rock cut her scalp to the bone.

Almost dear in her dumb persistence. When Maria howled
of being pricked with pins, slapped by invisible hands,
Miz Steele clutched her in whispering skirts and flailed
to beat off an unholy presence. It didn't work.
Nothing worked. Her hands as soft as pudding.

Nobody stopped food from going missing, or
the field hands' tools. Bottles of madeira danced.
Embers jumped from the hearth to bite ankles. The doctor
retreated to his fireless upstairs room, his rows of books
and guilty medicines. In the closet, a skeleton. Whose?

For peace, they sent Maria across water. Not the sea.
The muddy green of the Mississippi, supposed to short
her electricity. Clever spell they conjured, the sale
to Alabama. Some say she fell on the way and died.
Girl with a scar on her head, and what a mouth.

She lasted longer than Ellen, anyhow, who married young
out of the fancy carriage envied by neighbors. Unfolded
those red velvet steps, pranced down, and chronicles
mislaid her. Like Maria, who could negotiate with land itself,
persuade the stones to rise and heat and hurtle
in revolt. There are other powers, better, though
they may not get your name engraved in books. Some say
she acquired them. Returned to haunt the child she'd been,
head tied up in red, to stop the future burning through.

JOHN ROBINSON'S LIST, 1826

      This ruled and foxed document the only
      record of your name, followed by numbers
      firm and fat: three-hundred-twenty-five flat
      for Albert, age 13. Your face, nowhere.

Ma'am, you do not know the first thing.

      Persons bequeathed by Jockey Robinson
      to this university, along with a thousand
      acres at Hart's Bottom. A sepia squiggle
      ties you to Jerry, 53, and Elsey,
      36, blind. Your parents? Dick, Amorilla,
      Claiborne, Pompey, sisters and brothers?

I couldn't say
but it does look likely.

      Some of the entries hint at stories. Creasy,
      68, twenty dollars, but the note,
      in a column usually blank, offers a hard "worth
      nothing." The cursive relaxed but well-groomed.
      A breeze huffs at linen curtains. A pitcher
      sweats on the marble sideboard. How unworried
      the appraisal. How satisfied the gloss.

      Or thirteen names further, James the Preacher,
      40, costly, his wife Mary, their eight children,
      eldest five hired out, down to eight-year-old
      Isaac for five dollars a year. What did James
      preach about to Creasy-without-price,
      "club foot" Nero, and "lame" Dick McCollum?

Your son is thirteen. Would he listen
to a sermon or sleep right through?

    Are you like him? A quick boy, loves a game,
    strategizing always? I remember you,
    eyebrows hoisted, forehead grooved with notions.

No one gains by your imaginings.
Unless you do yourself.

    I can't find you on the 1834
    "List of Slaves Belonging to Washington College,"
    with Amorilla, Claiborne, Pompey, although
    I riffle all the bills. Eighteen months later
    Garland purchases nearly everyone
    to send to his Mississippi plantation:
    "Old Jerry was refused upon inspection."
    After the commission, trustees count
    twenty-two thousand dollars into coffers.
    That money translated to red brick buildings,
    lichened shady trees, and my salary.
    Is that how you linger, a ghost of ink
    boiled from walnut shells? A row of desks,
    a library shelf, digits propagating
    in some faraway white-pillared bank?

Ma'am, I cannot say.

BELLS FOR HENRY ALLEN

Dear Mr. Henry Allen,
	Before entering the archive, I read in other
papers about Alton Sterling, shot by police
in Baton Rouge. Father of Cameron, fifteen.
Same name and age as my son. Then I found you,
or a trace of you—a name on a list of people
bequeathed to my college in 1826.
Keep families together, the plantation owner
instructed the trustees, *farming Hart's Bottom
for fifty years*. The college contravened
his will. They sold your father, James the Preacher,
and his wife and younger children to pick cotton.
Bill of sale reads: *Henry retained, having a wife*.
You were twenty-six. Maybe you spoke
with a preacher's voice, a bell-resonance.
Power boosted by a hollow feeling.
	Records forget you till 1851.
January 6th, one Giles Gunn,
local teacher, wrote his sister Mary
of *a monstrous fuss… A letter was found in the road
purporting to be from one n— to
another… 300 men were to attack
the Military Institute and get possession
of the 20,000 stand of arms in the arsenal
there. Then they were to walk into the city
of Lexington killing all they could get
hold of. You had better believe that it made some stir.*
Local militia stepped up patrols. White
townsmen feared their so-called *servants*. City
Council addressed the university, *convinced
that Henry Allen, a slave, property of the College,*

is an unsafe negro, exerting over his fellows
*an influence highly prejudicial not to say
dangerous in the extreme, and believing as
we firmly do, that his longer continuance
in our midst would be productive of
incalculable evil.* They want him gone.
The word *incalculable* sprawls. Ink
darkens and the *request* gains urgent force.
Henry Allen's sale is <u>*loudly called for,*</u>
*and, for the promotion of the peace & quiet
of our town & the restoration
of wonted confidence around our firesides,*
<u>*imperiously* *demanded*</u>. The nib pressed down.
  The President authorized the Treasurer
to *dispose* of you to an alumnus in town.
Dr. Graham was a Jackson man,
outspoken, aggressive, who first opposed secession
then sent four sons to fight in gray. Your time
in that house, what was it like? Were you ever
freed? Of the rest of your days, no hint.
  Gunn thought the plot a hoax, perhaps by black
men, *to see what they could do.* The *Lexington
Gazette* agreed, but guessed *the negroes were frightened
more than the whites.* I think, Mr. Allen, that if
you wanted to strike, you would have struck without
warning patrols of your plans. If there ever was
a *letter in the road,* it was planted by white
secessionists, slavery's allies, intending
to scare into frenzy the placid Presbyterians,
some of whom pondered abolition.
  Your features a blur, but I guess if you worried
those comfortable men, it was for your watching eyes
at Sunday school, your sharp ears by the stables.

Your speech pealing, as if you could talk them sane.
      In your time, and since, and now, the argument
for destroying a black man's life is always
authorities thought him armed and meaning harm.
Death follows death, in terrible correspondence.
      The current college president declares
he won't apologize. I would say, if you
were willing to hear: the *incalculable evil*
was how men bought you, blamed you, traded you
away. I'm sorry they profited, and now I
profit, making and teaching words, while yours
went untranscribed. The silence still vibrates.
                Faithfully yrs.

"RECUMBENT LEE" BY EDWARD VALENTINE

Afflicted with frosty dreams, the marble man
reclines but keeps a hold of his saber. Notice
the clenched muscle above blanched brows.
Is appalled, maybe, by my fair daughter's
skimpy tank or the *fuck* she mutters, just
at the threshold of the docent's vigilance. Senses
a chill, now the chamber's stripped of flags.
A dreadful dust-web runs from nose-tip down
to mustache-bristle, but he still wears boots.
Pretending to rest. That blanket's the whitest of lies.

FIVE-STAR REVIEWS OF LEE CHAPEL

a found poem, after Aimee Nezhukumatathil

If you want to visit the grave of General Robert E. Lee, you better do it soon before the Libs dig him up
                Who knows how long it will remain undisturbed...?
the resting place of one of
if not the greatest leaders *[sic]* of all time.

The Washington & Lee campus…is about as southern as you can get...

One of the most beautiful and remarkable chapels in the Worlds. I am carried away every time…It is like nothing…

Whether you're a Yankee or a Southerner, Robert E. Lee is a man to be admired
                … almost unconditionally…

the prone marble sarcophagus is simply amazing
            it seems as if he is simply at rest, and not deceased …

Unfortunately the impressive recumbent
statue of Lee has been recently denuded
by the Washington & Lee administration
of the Confederate flags
        political correctness
        has recently ordered the removal of the two paintings…
        of Lee and Washington in full dress uniform, replacing
        them with new paintings of them in 'civilian' dress.
        That's just plain wrong.

Beeter *[sic]* go see this folks
   before most of it is removed due to liberalism and
      those who try to erase history.
         Staff told me it is already in the process…It's sad
            that my children may not be able to see history
               in the future

I suppose in today's political climate
that many would balk at visiting a place that honors a traitor

On the way out we tossed coins on Travellers grave
and were happy that we got here
before Antifa

BOIL-IN-BAG

*Brothers and sisters, there is nothing hateful
in showing pride for your rice. The liberals
have gone to a great deal of effort to make
refined grains feel ashamed. Join the fight
against husk, bran, and germ. Don't cede
this country's future to brown, to wild.*

It's funny like a conical hat, like
flaming crosses and assassination.
A vicious flier in a Ziploc, ballasted
by a milled and polished fistful, tossed
from a truck to my lawn. One grass to another.
Special triple K cereal. My counter-screed:
that baggie's a condom. Your racist seed, never
planted. Aborted before germination.

PAID ADVERTISEMENT

> *Because of all the trouble the democrats and black race are causing, I place this ad. No black people or democrats are allowed on my property until further notice.*
> —Raymond Agnor, *The News-Gazette*, July 15, 2015

The Judas trees are troubled. Purple blooms
long eaten by winds, woody seed-pods
coming on. No canker or coral-spot allowed
on these cordate leaves until further notice.

Lucy Long, Lee's other horse, long buried
on Mackey's farm, rolls her sad bones over.
The sorrel mare, steadier than his mount Traveller,
sends a ghost breeze whickering through the field.

No one seems to prickle when I limp down streets
named for generals. Register me a damp cloud.
First read of my body's party might be
mother, white. Not from here but allowed

on the grass, not a hue or sex shot on sight.
Privilege with a scent of condescension.
Because a threat riffles through my newspaper.
Unclassified. Some words can ionize.

Because new cattle underpass, football camp,
Auto Recyclers buying glass. A gust kicks up
where citizens dozed under flags, during
the killings. Charges me. I place this ad.

STATE ROADS

One route is Lee Street, named for Robert E., past the antebellum mansions and three-story pines, polishing brick pavements with your bootsoles, past the magnolia older than bees and shining hard, its branches a hoop skirt or cave for rage, past the only post office in the country not labeled *Post Office* because the locals loathed the feds as they still do, with or without raising a battle flag. Or consider a dirtier, unsanctioned path between Catholic Church and frat house, lined by dumpsters, past food-service guys smoking on the loading dock near the constricted concrete steps leading to the clinic, preferable not for what some call grit, but because the mud tells who has trudged that way, plus it keeps accepting signatures.

>today late snow gagged
>the daffodil mouths—
>but they kept yelling

FIRST BAPTIST, LEXINGTON

Paint is chipping from the ancestors.
Some stained glass broke and the steeple
needs repair. This church was built for people
who no longer pack boots and suspenders

into close wooden pews. Their arthritic hymn
can't lift to the barrel-vaulted ceiling.
Nobody home, is how the dead are feeling.
Instead of their heirs, me, heretic, from

elsewhere. Rolling off, the scions blurred
by sea-mist: ticketed travelers, angry sons
and disobedient daughters. Dislocation's
a birthright. Irreligion. You never heard

such a purple lily. So why sit here?
Because a wan lady from the historical
society is speaking of Diamond Hill,
now-rickety buildings risen in the east

where former slaves fitted beams of inns,
schools, homes. Because their children grew
up and sailed away. You never knew
such an absence, the disembodied incense.

Because my children gaze past the breakers
of the Blue Ridge. I linger because kids die
in Orlando, Aleppo, Chibok. There's too much why
not to pay heed. Here, in lieu of everywhere.

AMBITIONS

At Speed

I. *Are you famous?* demands the cabbie, careening across painted lanes and through swinging scarlet lights as he holds my eyes in the rearview mirror. *Okay, okay, nearly there, don't worry, never had an accident.*

II. Her laptop became a silver bird, flying up as the airplane dropped, passengers screaming. Another friend's wheelchair and rhinestones glitter. Another friend gone.

III. Ever coming and becoming.

IV. The moon this morning a thin-skinned clementine section, scented droplets suspended briefly in air.

V. He bowls his taxi down broad avenues, a gutter ball, no, straight down the middle, faster and faster, rattling time zones.

VI. Some days you pour out in chatter or in blood. Bottled months exsanguinate. Leave a stain and a tip, afraid he will not unlock the door.

VII. Terrible scroll of purple. Each word a mishap. Audience members feel ashamed.

VIII. No such thing as arrival. Only action. Wild roar as the wheels touch down but then you're running to the gate.

IX. Our luggage may have shifted in transit. Embarrassment's canister ruptures in the dark and there's hardly any left.

X. *So famous, very very famous,* you insist, *okay okay* he shouts, and laughter shakes your surviving friends. Nearly there.

THIS HAS GONE ON LONG ENOUGH

I need the number for my coffin, I mean
my loft, she says. Assisted living means
a studio choked with smoke and cat—
urine and musk—muddled with the human
tang of clothes not trusted to the laundry.
Back to Pittsburgh, she says. The time
has come. The reek and chime. She
isn't living. An elevator rises in a dream
she can only catch the scent of now:
independence of assistance. Window
green with plants. Lovers and their
cameras, their what was it, Rioja.
A lift sinks. Ash-tongue. This liquid is dry.
A dirty plot smells wrong. It's come, the time.

POSTLAPSARIAN SALSA VERDE

October, 2013

Sparrows and finches line nests with cigarette butts
shredded into fibers—nicotine wards off pests. It said so
in the paper. Now tacky fingers peel news from tomatillos,
sweet onions, cured garlic. What facts about the soiled world
can a person extract from the faintly striped rind of a broken
clove, oozing oil? Not that territorial politics starves
the government, Aimee unpaid, Jason on furlough—
that's just cellulose acetate accreting in the upside-down-cup
of my skull. Not how a baby suffers and her grandmother
shrinks beneath grief's heat, or how another friend
can't pay for help despite some health care revolution. Every
hope rusts or smokes. So I slide a tray of golden fruit
from the oven, onto the board, and watch steam condense
on a knife-blade. Scent of tart apples. Charred, they burst
into a hot mess of seeds and pulp, difficult to chop. Silent
on Syrian rebellion, on Marcia fasting before the surgery,
on empathetic elephants pointing with their trunks—these
papers delivering only the old report that making is hard.
Fingers burn. Boiling juice will trickle off the counter,
splash on bare feet. Read from an onion's brittle cover page:
there will be weeping. And change. And sweetness, only a mouthful,
after long labor. Tomatillos are a species of nightshade. Poison
in judicious doses deflects sorrow, or at least distracts
the eggheads at the table from pain's worm boring in.

LISTEN TO THE MOCKINGBIRD

May, 2016

She can sound like a hawk, a frog, crickets,
blue jay or car alarm. People don't like it

yet she sings less, and softer, than the male.
No sleeping in the valley when he rails.

Yes, she laid some alien eggs. Used
the wrong email server. Some calls, she rues.

But aren't all politicians mimics? Some want
a cardinal, showy, and his dun wife behind. One

or three songs with familiar lines. An honest
taste for lullaby, but let it rest.

The lilac wants her righteousness. When nestlings
hatch, she'll scream some hoary tuneless thing

as she strikes. Heard it over another girl's
grave, springs ago. Learned it pretty well.

INAPPROPRIATE

May, 2016

Worse than blood coming out of her
                                        wherever
is when it did but it's done and now, rather

than bake ginger snaps, she opens her lips.
Teeth in there.
                 No, you can't sit in her lap.

A pantsuit has campaigning to do. A pantsuit
spots an opening
                    in the White House.
                                  Calling the shots

from that lock she's got, the flesh gate, pink-lined
box with an heirloom pearl on top.
                           Some men mind

the very idea—someone in the Oval
they neither want to be
                    nor use. No girl.

No give. Not pretty or cane-sugar-sweetened, not dead
of shame, not yet. Not making
                        way. Just her bad

inhospitable secret vagina, delivering plans.
Can't see what she's got up there's
                           what they can't stand.

RESCUE BALLAD

June, 2016

There will be no authoritative
version. Ballads, like coal,
are found chiefly in mountains.
Not Florida wetlands, unfolded,

exposed. The pulse can be love
pressured by heat into hate.
No moral. No right side. Ballads
start at the end, are incomplete

without salsa and merengue.
Without rainbow strobes swirling.
So gather the flashes. The dancing.
Dissonance. A woman pushing

her son to safety. The shirtless boys
carrying the bleeding boys
to the street. Preserve the half-
forgotten, fugitive noise

of weeping mixed with singing. None
can recover the sense. Down
the petals crash and break. I'm sick
at heart and I want to lie down.

SITUATION ROOM

June, 2016

This isn't reality television, it's actual
reality, the candidate says from a virtual
stage. Behind her, flags, each star a symbol
of someone's home. Imagine, she says, Donald
in the situation room, making the call.
Life or death. Twitter and nuclear missile.
And, most concrete, a thousand miles of wall.
Does anyone pay for anything? For real,
her clashing blouse. Maybe spilled robot oil
on the softer one that polled well. Observable,
her training in how to punch a word, signal
feeling, join sturdy hands into a chapel.
Authentic, the YouTube ads. But presidential?
A feminine ending? How implausible.

INSIDE OUT

September, 2016

Shouldn't talk with a mouthful of half-chewed flags,
but he smirks and suggests her Secret Service guys
disarm and *see what happens*. The crowd turns wild
and you can spot a star wedged in his molar. Scraps
of stripe dangle from a lip. Maybe, he cracks,
the Second Amendment people will get wise.
While, you know, Russians hack her to bytes.
Silk between his teeth. Democracy. Facts.

Bleeding on the street's not too good for her,
thinks forty-plus percent of my broken
country. The liar calls her liar and the smear
sticks. After all, horror's ordinary. The thirteen-
year-old boy just killed for holding a BB gun.
And an open-mouthed woman—well, blood's her career.

CREDIT

October, 2016

Put this on her tab, jokes the mayoral candidate
ahead on line for groceries, waking me
from daydreams about a free-range chicken
roasting at home, good bread and greens. I laugh
generously, ask if he'll watch the debate tonight.
Exchanging words, each coin stamped with accord
about the world and passed back warm, until he
wheels off. My turn. Soon-to-be-mine chardonnay
and garnacha, six bottles for the discount. The cashier
surprises me, too. *Who do you think is going to win?*
I temporize: *The town hall?* He pauses to key
in cilantro. *Sure.* My mother taught me good manners,
meaning no religion, no politics, meaning smile,
meaning make people comfortable, never hungry,
never ashamed. My books taught me to speak, that
silence is disrespect. That it costs us all.
*Well, I keep waiting for Trump to cancel it, he's had such
a bad weekend.* Slow and calm, passing granola
across the scanner, a substantial man, he returns,
I don't think so. Now we are both trapped in a relation
that serves neither—troubled, perhaps he'll be in
trouble with his manager, anyone could hear this.
Yet I insist, *He said such terrible things.* The cashier,
to his credit, does not shrug. *All men talk like that,*
he says, *all men but God,* and next I know I'm
defending men, *not all, I know men who are shocked,*
as if men need my comfort, and perhaps he sees me
then filmed by a bubble of womanly innocence,

soap sheen reflecting protective dollar signs while
also mirroring with distortion his own face. *Kroger card?*
he asks and *Sorry, sorry,* I answer, dictating my digits,
inserting a silver flag in the chip reader, paying
with imaginary money for actual food, wondering
which of us ought to be kinder, knowing his feet
must ache, his hands look raw, but feeling like dirt,
like a *pussy,* to cash that word in, to be grabbed or
judged not fit for grabbing, disgusting forked
breastfeeding bleeding holder of unwelcome opinions
as I take my wealthy self back to a job where I serve
women and men who at least pretend to value me,
although I don't pretend to know what that's worth.

IMPERFECT TEN

November, 2016

My right eyelid has been twitching, as if to block defeat,
mildew spores, or cabinet appointments, since the election.

I cannot bear to hear men explain Clinton's failure
or how the Trump triumph makes sense, since the election.

Cannot bear to hear men speak at all. Especially tall
men—rich, white, straight men—since the election.

Is *intolerance* the word for what I'm feeling? Adrenaline
makes me ache. A craving for silence since the election.

I weigh 2.9 million pounds. Less than a person, yet fat
with fear. Hard pinch in the rustbelt since the election.

Hate crimes rise in schools and everywhere else. Anti-black,
anti-Muslim, anti-women, anti-immigrants, since the election.

Now it's *legal to grab you by the pussy,* said men in Colorado.
Pack your bags, shouted in class. Harassment since the election.

Hate beyond graffiti, bar chart, press release. Looking
for words under my feet, over the fence, since the election.

So here's a love song. Arab, Persian, Hindi, Pashto, Hebrew.
The ghazal an immigrant form I honor. Yet since the election,

I'm hopeless. Unloving of law, of walls, wheeling restlessly
past couplet's edge. None of us islands, since the election.

WORLD ORDER

With a blunt knife, cheap, he slices the out-
of-season apple, applying reasonable force,
thump, thump, and the hiss of cells torn open.

Window beside him a polite shade of blue,
not too, too, and the maple gracefully
expressing leaves so tender and appropriate.

This is a civil kitchen. No need to explain itself.
Gritty clouds of dust beneath the fridge vibrate
in silence. Onions too chilled for zing.

No news of what's mortgaged. Who ripped
that granite counter from what ground. Where
the apple grew. The grievous rain that swelled it.

HIBERNACULUM

Paper snowflakes, punchbowl, lecherous colleagues. A science-based
sun leaves the party early. Pissed off. Her allegations, evidence-based.

Lest she mount a solstitial harassment case, Mr. Entitlement
deducts words from her mouth. His trepidations, evidence-based.

Meanwhile, a chill propagates. Meanwhile, impeachment's a fetus
refusing birth and other deportations. Evidence-based

bacteria could violate its airtight NDAs. A virulent diversity
infect it. For that bad baby, no due date's in evidence. Based

on current models, however, he's doomed. All syllables will
    be transgender.
All punctuation will be fluid. Contamination will proceed with
    haste.

Talk dirty to us, change. Wheel like a season. Winter's always
    vulnerable
to sunlight's disclosure. Words do return. Their germination's
    evidence-based.

ALL-PURPOSE SPELL FOR BANISHMENT

A pox on _____ and the gerrymander
he rode in on. Expel, export, exile him
while we smudge sage-smoke around.
At this zero hour, as our wombs
contract under the moon, cast him out,
groper / loomer / cheater / rapist / harrassing
mogul bully frilled narcissus of a boss.
Evict without visa. Dissolve his assets
and social media accounts. Let there be no
comb-over strays stranded on sofa-backs,
no despotic perfume. Erase his name even
from rumor. From amygdala. Remove
all dimples left in moss by cloven loafer.
There is no _____. There never was.
As the last syllable of this incantation sounds,
it breaks over us how light we feel, like
lemon mousse in a silver dish on an early
spring morning before the leaves grow in,
each cell of foam trapping nothing but sugar
and sunshine. On our tongues, only _____.

AMBITIONS

Bath

I. So that my brother William Herschel may concentrate on becoming a famous astronomer.
II. Grind and polish mirrors, perform calculations, and wash lace cuffs. Read Alice B. Toklas while a mute swan drifts through reflections on the Avon.
III. Practice the stillness of the gilt head of Sulis, sleeping for centuries in a sewer.
IV. Pray to her for wisdom or at least the heat of the sun.
V. Consider prayer. A question etched on a lead tablet. Water wells up in reply. Whose water? What will happen if I drink?
VI. When my daughter the physics star was born, Hale-Bopp glowed in the sky. A maternity nurse wrapped me in blankets. We witnessed the brilliant tail.
VII. Pack cheese baps for the coach to Heathrow. Roll children's blouses neatly for cases. Be an ordinary woman. The sacred spring's water tastes of boiled eggs.
VIII. Be an ordinary comet-hunter. Consider how to gather available light, to see further.
IX. Track the celestial swan across a flawed glass while abbey bells bless some of us.
X. What equation could describe her orbit? Will anyone ever catch my shine?

IT'S STRIKING HOW MANY PEOPLE LOBBY THE CODE

Please help her walk this terrible corridor
in her new onions. Please confiscate his tears.
Bright rings of time, sliced, sting the onlooker.

It's nice that we can spend some temperature
together, she tries, although his visits are scarce.
He holds her arm as they stroll the corridor

together, on their way to lunch. Her hair
not so clean, no longer smart, but neat. Her fears
lightened by pills swallowed on time. No onlooker

would guess her Doctorate in Stats. The glamor
of grants, conference travel, buying art. Numbers
used to light her up. Now she walks the corridor

in unsteady measure. Doesn't track the hour.
Inserts, in talk's formulae, misfit words:
striking how. The funny sting. Any onlooker

might weep. Her son pretends to admire
the onions, not actually new, but still hers,
as much as anything. Please, corridor.
Time stings. Be bright for the onlooker.

INVOCATION

Bottomland: rouse. Sedge, knotweed:
time to rally. You've been lost
in thought, ebb and fuming flood,
since the glacier, thin winters
digging for turtles in cold mud.
Valley was tundra. Elk and moose
drank at water's brink while firs
invented shade. Panthers melted,

since then, into the dark, but spore
and mire could convene again.
Softness could still eat our footholds away.
Something here is thirsty for living's
every rivulet, hospitable and
treacherous in her oblivion.
Misty divots. Condensation
beading on throats, where pulses drum.

What kind of god is this? Her name
just a hieroglyph drawn in muck
by a tentative finger. No
answer but a hissing river.
Drowsy spirit, I'm pleading. Take
this blood shed unseasonably,
mineral gift. Be comfort. Be
danger. Of seep, of trough. Wake up.

PERIMENOPAUSE

Unstoppered. Uncorked. The spilt mess
of the body's plan puddles in the john,
useless now. Recurrence gone wrong.
Broken verses and a bloody chorus.

Who could have predicted red excess,
unspeakable clots of denouement?
My mouths are unjammed, endless mess
of me congealing at the bottom of the john.

Ready now to lose the losing: night sweats,
palpitations, insomnia, floods of gore, done.
Dried up, a long fluent speech in crimson.
Dissolved and flushed. Yet the song carries
on, uncorkable pour of me, shameless.

SONG OF THE EMMENAGOGUES

> *Vincent drank a potion Mother had concocted and walked and walked and walked.*
>   Norma Millay, quoted in Savage Beauty
>
> *I tell everybody how my mother feeds me on nettles and thistles, the heartless old thing.*
>   from Letters of Edna St. Vincent Millay

She was caught, fallen, over her time,
a blossomy month on the road.
Think and think twelve miles a day,
up and down hills near Shillingstone.

      Mugwort, nasturtium, rue,
      primrose, angelica, parsley.

The sun's clock ticked into summer
and down. Bigger than her sorrow.
Unmothering flower crouched in grass.
Scour the paths tomorrow.

      Henbane, gentian, all-heal,
      hyssop, thyme, bitter apple.

Some herbs provoke a woman's courses.
Says the book: decoct in wine.
The blue-petaled one, darling of Venus,
draws forth the undreamed-of child.

> Tea of the raspberry leaf. Ginger,
> cohosh, tansy, pennyroyal.

Refusal grew of her weeks in Dorset,
red-rooted alkanet in bloom.
Rhymes with secret, whisper the weeds.
Thatch hushes the cottages yet.

MILLAY AT FORTY-NINE

The freckled rover of weedy road and wave-
edge holed up for the winter in pajamas.
Pain knotted the hours but their jewel hues
relaxed when morphine pricked her blues. The way
to spring is so worn down, the warp's exposed.
Draw fretted blinds against the river views,
Fifty-Second Street's involved design. Gaze
inward at the rug: one arch, one rose.

Early sun can blanch the best, most perfected
pattern. Funds were tight, career come loose,
so she recorded verse in a faded voice.
It should have been a coup, her *Collected
Sonnets*, but the preface was beyond her.
The wool too bright. Too much skill to squander.

TURNING FIFTY IN THE CONFEDERACY

To live and die in Dixie was never
the plan. Old times here seemed best
forgotten, so down I plowed them.
Heritage, clay. Atrocity, clay.

Not secession; dispossession.
Long Island's where I was born,
three o'clock on a starry morning,
bleating an American hymn:

there is no here. *Away, away.*
At twenty-six, pitched what seemed
like camp in a Virginia valley.
First draft, provisional,

now set in sediment. There's shame
beneath my fingernails,
isotopic signature
of stolen soil in my bones.

I'm made of Dixie. Forgetting's
the trick of Daniel Emmett's air,
lifted from Ohio neighbors,
the Snowdens, black musicians.

Dixie may have been a Harlem
farmer who sold slaves south,
and one of them, name unsung,
composed that verse of yearning

to return. Story goes, the Lost Cause
anthem began as a wish
to slip north, passed from author
to fiddler to the white guy who

filed copyright. *Look away.* Years
wash past in silty muck. Can't carry
this tune; can't give it back.
Its burden stuck—become me.

SHE WILL NOT SCARE

Skunk under the wet bench
beside the aggrieved sea
through the drizzle before dusk
hushes in—you're sturdier
than self-doubt, than breakers

striping my unease. Inspirit me.
Give desire grit and legs.
Because the sea's too big,
lend me stench, your audacious,
insistent musk of indifference.

THE FERRY

By now I thought I'd be somewhere.
Hoped land would smudge the dim
distance. A wreath of smoke. A heap
of trophies, sexy legs entangled.

Instead, ambition's alone in a car,
parked on a rolling deck, hedged in
by other cars, an eighteen-wheeler.
Above the rail, cheerful water

glints, but a cement-mixer blocks
the sun. Forlorn tourists wander
the observation deck, peering
at horizons through heroic

lenses. Minimal visibility.
Clocking heads against the clouds.
I left my watch at the hotel.
My cell-phone bars are feeling down.

Sing it, waves. Rock the low, slow
passage that is hope sustained
by a nonchalant wink from the bay.
Nothing amazing will happen today.

SAYS THE CAB DRIVER OF THE APOCALYPSE

For protection against zombie hordes
you want a woman who's fed up with
bleeding, whose flint-spark eyes irradiate
your bone-strewn caves while she fixes
a peanut-butter sandwich. It's not
about skinny or baskets of decorative
gourds, not anymore, though famine
will harden her, though absence will
carve channels where once was pillow.
Much less about ammo and dominion.
Screw, or don't, the shaky sheriff who tries
not to be dickish. To hell with metabolic
yelling and facial scruff. You want—
hold on, these are slow, I'll just veer round
like so—you want a woman who knows
what the moon really thinks of you, says
well it's red, reflecting all our sunsets
or some such shit, now hurry let's *move*.

ENERGIZE

Transporter or holodeck? Either I
have rematerialized incompletely
(sparkling shower of particles
dimmer) or this simulated city

has acquired a wobble, a tell.
Puffy-jacketed people
duck from awning to overhang
along Newbury Street wondering

if swan boats sail in the slanting
drizzle or a hand-held foam-coated
reservoir might suit better. Inside
the Church of the Covenant,

meanwhile, Tiffany glass
somehow glows against cold
puddingstone—how does a yoked
god's robe luminesce by cloud,

its whiteness alive with ocher
and smoky motion? Gazing
at invisible sparrows, bracing
an overlarge hand on a rock,

he is surely transported too,
that blink of tropical foliage
behind him now, a dreamy blue,
and him thinking how, lord,

did I get to Boston? I drove,
theoretically, via the hospital
where nurses unhooked my mother
from catheter, from I.V.,

and handed her over. Moved
a bed downstairs, stocked her fridge
with little bottles of virtual
food optimistically labeled

Ensure for safety and, for power,
Boost. Counted and sealed
her pills into rows of labeled
oyster shells. Then, north,

as if stillness were heresy.
Back home a library of mountains
I never read. Mosaic rain
I smash right through.

Look at the god, good-looking,
how he looks at the ground,
willing it real, willing himself
to love where he hardly lives,

in his stupid human body,
an always ailing thing. Rather
the sparrow be true than cells
struggling to contain

unlikely radiance, and failing.
Compounding errors. The tumor
an index of poisons, every one
chiming as they transform her.

OLD BAG

The opposite of reincarnation
turns me upside down like a
pillowcase. Spirit feathers spill.

Body wrinkles and pouches,
unwilling to release the final
hieroglyphic trickle of quills.

I tell anecdotes about myself
to make a self and hate to let
the ink shaft empty out. Oh,

those linty corners. Oh, the stain
at the navel of the cheap
wineglass. Even as you wipe

away the last distressing hairs,
the tub fills with water. Lonely girl
got drunk to the dregs. Angry

woman kicked her basket over
and all that's left of vegetables
are broom-straw-streaks of soil

on her floor. Now my children
are packing their cases while I
nest snacks in the last lunch sacks.

Enough of the mother-coop. Unhem
me, let those fabrications go, even
sunset's sentimental afterglow.

This skin remembers myths that tried
to stand like water, incubate. Joints
know how certain tales wanted

to mulch down like roots of a vanished
tree persisting in the ground. Fighting
the future's occupation. Fingers say

dig that grit out of the shoe. Flesh
and brain a reusable tote, filthy,
frayed. Let its emptiness be

new. Let winter's bright wind brim it.

STATE FRUIT

Soursop, yellow maddening to green,
resolute berry that kicks the ground,
hard star falling reluctantly.
Sour-hearted pulp, locked in green
for obstinate weeks. Then, scent. Seeds
jingle. Custard's plush in the mouth.
Sweetsop changed to purple-green,
gone strange: solved fruit, kind ground.

AMBITIONS

Lexington

I. Live where I live, this earth, this body.
II. Remember what Virginia bluebells tell, aching tales by the swollen Maury.
III. Listen to the hindering question: —whence the need, as Margaret Junkin Preston asked, when the world is over-deaved with speech?
IV. Not to soothe her Confederates, or not, at least, hatred's blister. But any body has many wounds, needs kind doctors, outlandish salves.
V. Poke memory-nests with any stick I can reach until the pollinators fly. No bloom without bees, although I fear the sting.
VI. Stories that are not my story reinvent me.
VII. Few humid days without a thunderstorm: insistent breeze, clouds unleashing feeling. Flashes of illumination. Furious rain that saves me.
VIII. Mercy, not forgiveness. Unblame the pouching belly and stiff joints, how spring's azure candles fail before will's consummation. Guilty, unshriven, but deserving mercy.
IX. Unblame flaggers, abusive bosses, gods who will not wake up. Unblame clay that sticks when I want to move and chokes what I want to grow. Mercy upon them.
X. Call down sanctions to flood, to wash me away. Always I was meant to be wrack in the morning, stranded and damp. Whether or not they have the right to bless, bluebells ring and ring.

EVAPORATIVE HAIBUN

Back at the trailhead, spring was just an aspiration: winter-wrecked nest, cool bulb stirring in soil. Then came long rains. Now, on the path from speechless limbs to green postcards, even the lilac is getting ideas. Which is not to imply small beauties suffice. On another road, migrant caravans are massing. In the stream, pollutants foam. Friends reel through illness, the way itself difficult to see, pretty finches a mockery. But a person wants to say. But a person wants to try. To spend the prickly minutes anticipating peonies. A lush dream of roses growing indoors, climbing the trellis of the bed, drawing bees. Because all trails loop—

> even the river—
> although most of us can't climb
> cloud-wise

NO HERE HERE

Podunk, like Atlantis, has no locus.
Boston Herald, *1933*

Where am I? Middle of a jerkwater town,
the rails yanked up. Straining against a pretty
mediocrity. Unfitted to my skin.

Call it Nowheresville. My valley, vacuity.
My pulse turned desperate. So comes the beige
room, technicians, detector, chest cavity

bared by an X-ray pulse that writes a page
devoid of answers. Heart stranded between
shudders. Map of my gaps and forking veins.

I am afraid. I err. Winter rain
spatters the dormant trees, the bloated river,
refusing to change into spring's inspiration—

nohow, nowise—or apocalypse either.
Time eddies. Studies suggest. Two out of three
doctors say calm down: it's nothing, or

it's hormones. I wander, no chart, no key.
Somewhere close, unmarked on parchment, a shade
shifts across rocks, unmoored from the tree.

A wolf-shaped darkness stalks it. Neither is saved
because no genius loci haunts these outlandish
boondocks. Limbo under eclipse. No guide,

no god with a name in a surviving language.
Invocation's rites not meant for me. Yet
hear *boondock* again: the word's Tagalog

for *mountain*. Grasses creep across the flats
even in Siberia, synonym
for exile. Podunk, Algonquin, that's

place where you sink. Maybe I'll summon
a backwater spirit of dubious power as, here
in the sticks, stiff sap struggles to thrum

through channels. Start at the root. Pray by ear.

INSATIABLE

The tide wants in,
each wave a cave of desire.
To touch sand's skin,
the tide heaves in
from valleys of famine.
How distant the shore
when the combers roll in,
grown hollow with desire.

MEDITATION

Ivy worries the dying tree. Robins
worry the grass, which is hardly grass
but an audience of violets mimicking
the sky. Mist worries the mountain,
a neckache of twisted pearls.
All the little screens are worried by light
and scripts of darkness squirming
across the light. Melting permafrost
should worry everyone, a toxin
of dread polluting bodies that sleep
badly, eat expensively, and spend too
many hours in chairs working on nothing
important, and of course I mean mine.
I wonder, as I worry sentences, whether
worry could be an expression of anger.
Only land knows the answer, bedrock
of sedimented loss, shawled and crawled
over by strivers and their excrements,
strapped down by pavements, thinking so
slowly about us all and refraining from bringing
the topic around to itself every damn time
because it is time, breathless and all breath,
a vital feeling that knows itself unworryable.

CAVE PAINTER, DORDOGNE

After sketching ten thousand churning forelegs
in river sand—after hunt, slaughter, dinner
taught lessons in muscle and bone—your hand
has earned the curve of a bison's back.

Fat is smeared in concave rocks to burn
with juniper wicks; you've powdered ochre,
chewed a bit of hide soft for a sponge.
No longer young. Every joint groans

while you climb the scaffolding. Then,
as pupils slowly widen, you forget
the smoking griefs and pursue shadow.
Whole herds await release. That stalactite,

a tail. Rocky dimple, a horse's belly:
starved to the touch, but to the eye, as replete
with secrets as a mare in foal. Next
blow a mist of pigment through hollow bone

and each sooty line is true the first time.
That third-best aurochs might survive
seventeen thousand years while its livelier kin
wash down a wall, silting like ghosts into

la Vézère, but on a good day you don't care.
Finding can be happier than keeping.
What I can't fathom is where you hope
they're going, the queues of rusty bulls

and horses. Or is it the same horse, over
and over, in motion? It leaps into the dark,
or flows. Each beast with work
to unearth, deep in the limestone.

HOUSE CALL

The black fox kept eluding me,
quick among the party shoes,
chrysanthemum scent of twilight
blowing through lamplit rooms.
Its fur was tipped with flame,
brushed by crimson characters.
Out the door, down the steps
to mist-damp grass. Gone, gone
under sharp-leaved rhododendrons.

What did you bring me, kitsune?
Twigs and dead matter   Come sleep
Where are you now? *Under your nails*
your skin   flashing through veins
Will I be fortunate? *This dream*
is your luck   this restlessness
You feared warm rain had ceased falling—
that the onion moon had rolled
beyond night's uneven floor.

Try to read spirit and this
ensues: writing shivers, a trick,
a tease. Creatures shifting shape
can't pause at the mirror to preen.
Someone wears nine tails;
something prepares to change
by burning all the words.
A smoke of fox escapes.

PUSHING TOWARD THE CANOPY

When I wave, the neighbor turns away.
A lichened oak branch broke three stories up;
summer-dark leaves shake in the rain.
I don't know what I'm doing again.

The dangling branch tells three old stories:
*Sapwood channeled my desire. I'm high
and don't know what I'm doing, again.
Ambition transformed into heartwood.*

My sapwood rose and became me while
the ground mulled over water, water.
Any hardening heart could change its vote.
Rain, unwanted, runnels the dirt.

Too much water can weigh you down
till your summer-dark leaves shake with strain.
What do I want, if not dirt and rain,
and friends who turn to me and wave?

SPIRALS

Even on the street, I am in the forest.
Mornings when I pass the condemned
apartments, now housing kudzu and opossum,

tendrils touch my cheek with alien ambition,
vines stretching farther every day, across
the sidewalk, now the road, vibrating.

Even waking, I am dreaming, although
I tamp it down in the name of decision.
That baby, how was she my responsibility?

Her pincer grip kept sliding over the pink-
and-gold fruit I cubed for her. She was not
real, but I carried her damp, heavy ghost

to the post office, the voting booth. If only
more could see the forest containing
the asphalt—could hear the dreams hum

in daylight. Words that seem reasoned
are full of rustling creepers. A trance can startle
you aware, but only for a little curl, a why.

FEELING GOOD

Maybe they get off that way, although the posture can't
result in a baby panda: Mei Xiang flat as half-melted snow
during this one fertile day per year, rump too low
for Tian Tian's access, so he climbs up her foothills
and stands on her back, triumphant. Sexually
inventive zoologists built a platform in the bears'
favorite candlelit bamboo grove, hoping she'd trip
and land at an inviting angle and, holy romance, she did,
but chivalrous Tian Tian lifted her, she pancaked
alluringly, and he posed on her back again. The keepers
sighed like spring wind through pine needles.
All the keepers, yours and mine, are sighing.
Today, on Panda Cam One, a two-toned sleeper
in a dim enclosure. Nose almost touches knees. Belly
rises, belly sinks. A midnight paw twitches like my own
hand on the pillow. Click a link and see the other
half-reclined against a painted backdrop of mountains.
He or she gnaws at leafy shoots, thinking of obduracy
and desire. There are many pleasures, most of them
stupid. Fullness. Oblivion. The view from another animal's
shoulders, or low down in the dew, when every furry particle
yields to gravity's persistence, gives up, gives out, gives in.

BORDER SONG

for Jenna and Lucy

While two brides weep, strings of origami
flutter from a staged gate to a genuine pond.

The person with the guitar pauses, listening,
and wind whispers into the microphone.

Three geese ride currents over our heads,
witnessing the witnesses, also weeping.

Not far away, on the island's shore,
the steely rollers strum themselves. In love.

Everything shines, the water, the music,
the hour's edge. Everybody resonates.

Leaves dangle, pale handkerchiefs. All kisses
percuss, turning isolate sounds around to face

each other. Eager to bless, wind taps the mike
again, hikes a breath, calls them in.

WE COULD BE CYBORGS

Since the doctor carved his eyeball and
inserted a toric lens, his glance glitters
differently. Pale as winter or a bank
of chill machines. Since her throat constricted,
she lies wakeful, tuned to the bloody clash
of prednisone jitters and strong-armed melatonin,
reminded of the Tasman and Pacific
straining at each other's seam. Natural,
at this age, to decay and disjoint—to seek
chemical solder and replacement parts.
The genre has changed from romance to science
fiction, with change itself the charismatic
star. Cyborgs like quiet, but that's obsolete.
This is love to the limits, at flickering speed.

NATIVE TEMPER

Some call the maple a trash tree, the landscaper said,
kicking what remained of a ground-down stump.
Sawdust bleached the laurels, already near-dead

of drought and neglect. *But they grow fast enough
you'd see the prime of it. And autumns, they just blaze.*
Between shovel-pokes at fibrous roots, he weighed up

the relative assets of laidback hickories
and other slow locals—maybe a pin oak or, well,
he'd leave us to consider a few more days.

The last, lost maple was broken by the gale
of my father's death. All that mystery
laid bare. Studied on the wound awhile until,

three May leaf-counts past, anyone could see
it was tired of fighting. Guys came with a crane
and piteous saws. I grieve that missing tree

more than my old man. *Some folks will choose a kind
only their children can know the whole grandness of,*
mused the good citizen. Yet I have a stump to grind

with the South. An invasive species, at heart.
My kids should leave. Plant something flashy, I said.
I would rather die than die in these parts.

LIVE FROM THE SURFACE OF THE MOON

The landing leg (*porch*) jets
a web of shadows across lunar
powder while brilliantly bleached
astronauts lope across the frame

On Sunday July 20th 1969
I am not yet two : : do not divine
how the moon mirrors the sun
and the *magnificent desolation*

of a Rockland County building site
bald of grass : : each split-level home
a lunar module far from inflation
Vietnam race riots assassination

I cannot possibly remember thirty-
plus hours with Walter Cronkite and
Wally Schirra : : parents buzzing
as transmissions crinkle and flicker : :

much less an animation of the Eagle
advancing toward the Sea of Tranquility
or shots of the LEM's quadruped replica
in Bethpage Long Island : : bug face

with a long metal snout between
wide black reflective window eyes
(choked-up Cronkite says *those kids
who are kind of pooh-poohing this thing*

I'd like to know what they thought

*at this moment when our mouths
were in our throat* : : *How can anyone
turn off to a world like this*)

With one-sixth of adult gravity
I bound through oversized rooms
careful not to jag my special suit
on an exposed martini glass : : every

high-altitude glance or word
a UFO : : *'One small step for man'*
the anchor explains *but I didn't get
the second phrase* : : until static

lulls me to sleep : : The grown-ups
tip themselves into a queen-size
while Aldrin and Armstrong tuck
each other in on an airless satellite

perhaps under yellow foil blankets
but how could I know : : each maybe-
memory overwritten now like
boot prints in moondust

by footage on my little screen
(who would have thought the future
would be *small*) : : What I carry out
in my sample bag is not mankind leaping but

a nightmare : : Giant mechanical
spiders chasing me across the dead
land : : I lope to a quilted islet
hop up on the shadowy porch : : only

my groggy parents do not want me
Precarious love : : Any moonman might
splash down safely and find home
isn't safe and never really was

ILLUMINATED

Loopy with delight, I practiced
cursive not on boys' surnames
but on my favorite letter.
Symbol for large, language, lesbian.
In a ship's log, lightning.
Fifty, elevated, low gear, liberated.
Love the eye up high,
knot left loose beneath. Last,
never least, thrust tongue against
palate and teeth. Now, release.

NEW YEAR COLONOSCOPY

The procedure went swiftly, dark falling early,
whirling into the back of my hand like snow
in gigantic, ornamental flakes, first one
melting against blood's heat, then others
sticking cold, ganging up against my will
to worry, a blanket of anesthetic hush; then,
although I could not feel it and do not remember,
a sexist Republican doctor pried a scope
through my back door, probing for regret,
dangerous thoughts, the kind that over time
grow bulbous, serrate; but he found nothing,
no secrets, no intention to accrue them, for I
boiled the bones and drank the steam,
sipped pink potions hours on end, emptied
myself of last year's toxic shit, and am clean.

L

1967 was on fire: Apollo 1 waiting to launch / Jim
Morrison on Ed Sullivan stoking it *higher* / Mekong
Delta / Newark riot hurling out sparks / summer of
o sock it to me sock it to me sock it to me sock /
pulsar first glimpsed black hole first named / far
south Deception Island's volcano in flames / while
an infancy rages / some recently extinguished soul
was slotted in my pigeonhole (Oppenheimer Coltrane
Magritte) / but I'm no reincarnate star not even a
meteor tail (Toklas) / just a minor cloud of space
dust reborn to squall anew / Four decades & change
accrue & a big birthday looms / half & half golden
jubilee 5-0 code for pigs closing in & also atomic
number of tin / Mystery heat rises to scald / What
is it I'm reaching for over this terrible wall / A
relocation / destination / permission for ignition
because beauty burns low / potential guttered long
ago / I don't know / So I avoid mirrors except the
page and work / burn the fuel of myself in words /
program words to change this space & time / Recall
Cobain & Philip Seymour Hoffman dissolved to smoke
/ Does it even matter how in that year of our new-
born howl Lou Reed crooned *heroin* into the cradles
/ o it was a Warhol year surreal bananas / From my
room painted like late-in-the-daylily / I can gaze
across a blank tin roof pocked by finch claws past
snow-packed sockets of a desolate maple toward the
lavender brow of House Mountain that for this poem
let's personify as Ambition / the blaze considered
discourteous to mention especially by women / Well
shouldn't I be striving? / Talk to me Mountain / &

with a higher perspective than mine Mountain cries
/ *You are a conflagration* / *Adrenaline singes your
capillaries* / *Let the anniversary of your ardor to
be born cool you like a shadow* / *Desire leads only
to more desire even were your sororal motives pure
and they are not* / *Mountain has spoken!* / It meant
cease building with borrowed stones unless to lift
somebody else / message over bottle / *O & hey* says
Mountain *one more thing* / *All poems may be ash but
some shelter small hot hopes* / *their seed swaddled
in earth's velvet* / What strikes me now like flint
on tinder is how talking to mountains or to you is
the same as talking to myself / just as impossible
& just as hopeful / either / or / both / & / Maybe
we're all alpine & none of us is / disconnection a
gift of language we are supposed to hand back / No
presents please what's yours is mine already / But
come in & have a drink on me / Today's everybody's
birthday & I've stopped counting / well just about

NOTES

"American *Incognitum*" owes details to Elizabeth Kolbert's *The Sixth Extinction* (Henry Holt, 2014).

"Racketing Spirits" draws from a tale recounted by Anne Brandon Heiner in the proceedings of the Rockbridge Historical Society, Volume 7, 1966-1969 (10-22); Oren F. Morton's *A History of Rockbridge County, Virginia* (McClure Company, 1920); and J. Lewis Peyton's *A History of Augusta County, Virginia* (Samuel L. Yost and Son, 1882).

"John Robinson's List" was inspired by documents posted on the timeline "African Americans at Washington and Lee," including a 2007 honors thesis for the History Department written by Emma Burris (Janssen), *An Inheritance of Slavery: The Tale of "Jockey" John Robinson, His Slaves, and Washington College*. "Bells for Henry Allen" includes fact and speculation from those sources and the *Lexington Gazette* (January 23rd, 1851); the Giles Gunn collection of the Virginia Military Institute; and the 1851-2 Trustee papers archived in Special Collections at Washington and Lee University. It was drafted in July, 2016.

"Boil-in-Bag" misquotes a racist flier tossed onto my lawn during the spring of 2015, in a plastic bag weighted with white rice.

"Rescue Ballad" is indebted to *Traditional Ballads of Virginia*, edited by Arthur Kyle Davis, Jr. (University Press of Virginia, 1929), as well as to *New York Times* coverage of the Pulse nightclub mass shooting in Orlando, Florida.

"Song of the Emmenagogues" and "Millay at Forty-Nine" are informed by Nancy Milford's biography of Edna St. Vincent Millay, *Savage Beauty* (Random House, 2001); *Letters of Edna St. Vincent Millay,* ed. Allan Ross Macdougall (Harper & Bros., 1952); *Culpeper's Complete Herbal* (W. Foulsham & Co., Ltd., 1880); Angus McLaren's *A History of Contraception* (Basil Blackwell, 1990); and John M. Riddle's *Eve's Herbs* (Harvard, 1997).

"Turning Fifty in the Confederacy" contains phrases from "Dixie," a song published by Daniel Decatur Emmett in 1860. Also see *Way Up North in Dixie: A Black Family's Claim to the Confederate Anthem* by Howard L. Sacks and Judith Rose Sacks (University of Illinois Press, 2003).

"Ambitions: Lexington" quotes "The Good of It" by Margaret Junkin Preston, from *Cartoons* (Roberts Brothers, 1875).

ACKNOWLEDGMENTS

About Place: "Paid Advertisement," "Rescue Ballad"
Barrow Street: "Ambitions: Liverpool," "Recumbent Lee"
Beloit Poetry Journal: "Dear Anne Spencer"
Blackbird: "Pushing toward the Canopy"
CDC Poetry Project: "Hibernaculum"
Cascadia Subduction Zone: "Racketing Spirits"
Cave Wall: "Invocation," "No Here Here"
Cherry Tree Review: "Perimenopause," "This Has Gone On Long Enough," "Boil-in-Bag," "Native Temper"
Cimarron Review: "Inside Out"
Cold Mountain Review: "Before Lexington," "American Incognitum"
The Common: "Meditation"
Copper Nickel: "Cave Painter, Dordogne"
Ecotone: "Turning Fifty in the Confederacy," "State Song"
Flock: "John Robinson's List, 1826," "Evaporative Haibun"
Gettysburg Review: "L"
Hampden-Sydney Poetry Review: "Bells for Henry Allen"
Interim: "Ambitions: Bath," "Ambitions: Lexington," "Visibility Poor"
Kestrel: "Insatiable," "Selfish," "The Ferry"
Manifest West: "Fifty-Fifty"
Mezzo Cammin: "Millay at Forty-Nine," "Song of the Emmenagogues"
National Poetry Review: "State Fruit" as ("Pawpaw")
New Ohio Review: "Uncivil," "World Order"
Notre Dame Review: "Traces," "Live from the Surface of the Moon"
Ocean State Review: "Border Song"
One: "Postlapsarian Salsa Verde"
Poet Lore: "Spirals"

Poetry Northwest: "Fire Ecology," "It Is Striking How Many People Lobby the Code"
Queen of Cups: "House Call"
Raintown Review: "Situation Room"
Rise Up Review: "Imperfect Ten," "Inappropriate"
Salamander: "All-purpose Spell for Banishment"
storySouth: "First Baptist, Lexington," "Spring Rage"
Sweet: "Feeling Good"
SWWIM: "Energize"
TAB: A Journal of Poetry and Poetics: "Old Bag"
Tahoma Literary Review: "Ambitions: At Speed"
Talking Writing: "We Could Be Cyborgs"
Terrain.org: "The South"
Unsplendid: "Occulted Sonnet" (as "Past Meridian")
Water-Stone Review: "Illumination"

"Pushing Against the Canopy" was featured on *Poetry Daily* on January 1, 2018, and "Inside Out" was featured on *Verse Daily* on July 15, 2019. "Black Walnut Tree" was commissioned by Rose McLarney and Laura-Gray Street for *A Literary Field Guide to Southern Appalachia* (University of Georgia Press). "Song of the Emmenagogues" appears in *Choice Words: Writers on Abortion,* edited by Annie Finch (Haymarket Press). "The South" appears in *Dear America,* edited by Simmons Buntin, Elizabeth Dodd, and Derek Sheffield (Trinity University Press). "*En Dehors Garde* Bingo" appears in the online project *Mina Loy: Navigating the Avant-Garde* as part of a feminist theory "flash mob" via digital postcard. "State Fruit" (as "Pawpaw") was featured in Carillion's *Poems in the Waiting Room* series, edited by Sandee McGlaun.

I am very grateful to many editors for shining a light on these poems and, in some cases, for advice. Thanks also to the people at *Sweet,* who nominated "Feeling Good" for a Pushcart Prize in 2017 and Best of the Net in 2018; *Flock,* for nominating "John Robinson's List" for a Pushcart in 2018; and *Rise Up Review,* for nominating "Imperfect Ten" for *Bettering American Poetry.*

The staff of Special Collections at Washington and Lee University was generous to me as I researched these poems, especially Tom Camden and Lisa McCown. Their assistance enriched my understanding of local history; any errors are mine. Lenfest Grants at Washington and Lee helped fund my work.

Boundless thanks to Chris Gavaler, Janet McAdams, Nathalie Anderson, and Molly Sutton Kiefer, who read earlier versions of this book and gave counsel and encouragement. Alston Cobourn Brake, Leah Green, Ellen Mayock, Deborah Miranda, Seth Michelson, and Beth Staples gave useful advice on individual poems. Thanks also to the support and inspiring examples of friends in and beyond 50 Ways Lexington, especially Ellen, Tinni, Stephanie, Theresa, and Other Ellen. Without them, turning fifty under a poisonous administration, amid the remains of the Confederacy, would have been far nastier.

Lesley Wheeler's four previous poetry collections include *Radioland* and *Heterotopia*, which was winner of the Barrow Street Press Poetry Prize; her first novel is *Unbecoming*. Poetry Editor of Shenandoah, she blogs at lesleywheeler.org, tweets as @LesleyMWheeler, and teaches at Washington and Lee University in Lexington, Virginia.